This book belongs to:

Contact Details:

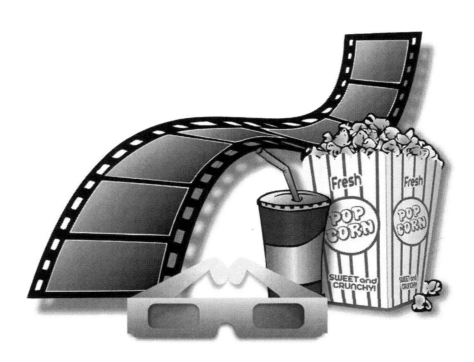

Movies To Watch

Title	Main Actor	Genre	Year

Movies To Watch

Title	Main Actor	Genre	Year

Movies To Watch

Title	Main Actor	Genre	Year

Movies To Watch

Title	Main Actor	Genre	Year

MOVIE:

Director:

Date Released:

Written by:

Genre:

Actors:

My Review

MEMORABLE SCENE

MEMORABLE QUOTE

My Rating:
☆☆☆☆☆

PAGE NO:

MOVIE:

Director:

Date Released:

Written by:

Genre:

Actors:

My Review

MEMORABLE SCENE

MEMORABLE QUOTE

My Rating:

☆☆☆☆☆

PAGE NO:

MOVIE:

Director:

Date Released:

Written by:

Genre:

Actors:

My Review

MEMORABLE SCENE

MEMORABLE QUOTE

My Rating:
☆☆☆☆☆

PAGE NO:

MOVIE:

Director:

Written by:

Actors:

Date Released:

Genre:

My Review

MEMORABLE SCENE

MEMORABLE QUOTE

My Rating:

☆☆☆☆☆

PAGE NO:

MOVIE:

Director:

Date Released:

Written by:

Genre:

Actors:

My Review

MEMORABLE SCENE

MEMORABLE QUOTE

My Rating:
☆☆☆☆☆

PAGE NO:

MOVIE:

Director:

Written by:

Actors:

Date Released:

Genre:

My Review

MEMORABLE SCENE

MEMORABLE QUOTE

My Rating:
☆☆☆☆☆

PAGE NO:

MOVIE:

Director:

Date Released:

Written by:

Genre:

Actors:

My Review

MEMORABLE SCENE

MEMORABLE QUOTE

My Rating:
☆☆☆☆☆

PAGE NO:

MOVIE:

Director:

Date Released:

Written by:

Genre:

Actors:

My Review

MEMORABLE SCENE

MEMORABLE QUOTE

My Rating:

☆☆☆☆☆

PAGE NO:

MOVIE:

Director:

Written by:

Actors:

Date Released:

Genre:

My Review

MEMORABLE SCENE

MEMORABLE QUOTE

My Rating:
☆☆☆☆☆

PAGE NO:

MOVIE:

Director:

Date Released:

Written by:

Genre:

Actors:

My Review

MEMORABLE SCENE

MEMORABLE QUOTE

My Rating:

☆☆☆☆☆

PAGE NO:

MOVIE:

Director:

Date Released:

Written by:

Genre:

Actors:

My Review

MEMORABLE SCENE

MEMORABLE QUOTE

My Rating:

☆☆☆☆☆

PAGE NO:

MOVIE:

Director: _____   Date Released: _____

Written by: _____   Genre: _____

Actors: _____

My Review

_____
_____
_____
_____
_____
_____
_____
_____
_____
_____
_____
_____
_____
_____
_____
_____
_____
_____
_____
_____
_____
_____
_____
_____
_____
_____
_____
_____

MEMORABLE SCENE

_____
_____
_____
_____
_____
_____
_____
_____

MEMORABLE QUOTE

_____
_____
_____
_____
_____
_____
_____

My Rating:

☆ ☆ ☆ ☆ ☆

PAGE NO:

MOVIE:

Director:

Date Released:

Written by:

Genre:

Actors:

My Review

MEMORABLE SCENE

MEMORABLE QUOTE

My Rating:

☆☆☆☆☆

PAGE NO:

MOVIE:

Director:

Date Released:

Written by:

Genre:

Actors:

My Review

MEMORABLE SCENE

MEMORABLE QUOTE

My Rating:
☆☆☆☆☆

PAGE NO:

MOVIE:

Director:

Date Released:

Written by:

Genre:

Actors:

My Review

MEMORABLE SCENE

MEMORABLE QUOTE

My Rating:
☆☆☆☆☆

PAGE NO:

MOVIE:

Director:

Date Released:

Written by:

Genre:

Actors:

My Review

MEMORABLE SCENE

MEMORABLE QUOTE

My Rating:
☆☆☆☆☆

PAGE NO:

MOVIE:

Director:

Date Released:

Written by:

Genre:

Actors:

My Review

MEMORABLE SCENE

MEMORABLE QUOTE

My Rating:

PAGE NO:

MOVIE:

Director:

Date Released:

Written by:

Genre:

Actors:

My Review

MEMORABLE SCENE

MEMORABLE QUOTE

My Rating:

☆☆☆☆☆

PAGE NO:

MOVIE:

Director:

Date Released:

Written by:

Genre:

Actors:

My Review

MEMORABLE SCENE

MEMORABLE QUOTE

My Rating:
⭐⭐⭐⭐⭐

PAGE NO:

MOVIE:

Director:

Date Released:

Written by:

Genre:

Actors:

My Review

MEMORABLE SCENE

MEMORABLE QUOTE

My Rating:

☆☆☆☆☆

PAGE NO:

MOVIE:

Director:

Date Released:

Written by:

Genre:

Actors:

My Review

MEMORABLE SCENE

MEMORABLE QUOTE

My Rating:

⭐☆☆☆☆

PAGE NO:

MOVIE:

Director:

Written by:

Actors:

Date Released:

Genre:

My Review

MEMORABLE SCENE

MEMORABLE QUOTE

My Rating:
☆☆☆☆☆

PAGE NO:

MOVIE:

Director:

Date Released:

Written by:

Genre:

Actors:

My Review

MEMORABLE SCENE

MEMORABLE QUOTE

My Rating:
☆☆☆☆☆

PAGE NO:

MOVIE:

Director:

Date Released:

Written by:

Genre:

Actors:

My Review

MEMORABLE SCENE

MEMORABLE QUOTE

My Rating:

☆☆☆☆☆

PAGE NO:

MOVIE:

Director:

Date Released:

Written by:

Genre:

Actors:

My Review

MEMORABLE SCENE

MEMORABLE QUOTE

My Rating:
☆☆☆☆☆

PAGE NO:

MOVIE:

Director:

Date Released:

Written by:

Genre:

Actors:

My Review

MEMORABLE SCENE

MEMORABLE QUOTE

My Rating:
☆☆☆☆☆

PAGE NO:

MOVIE:

Director:

Date Released:

Written by:

Genre:

Actors:

My Review

MEMORABLE SCENE

MEMORABLE QUOTE

My Rating:

☆☆☆☆☆

PAGE NO:

MOVIE:

Director:

Date Released:

Written by:

Genre:

Actors:

My Review

MEMORABLE SCENE

MEMORABLE QUOTE

My Rating:

☆☆☆☆☆

PAGE NO:

MOVIE:

Director:

Date Released:

Written by:

Genre:

Actors:

My Review

MEMORABLE SCENE

MEMORABLE QUOTE

My Rating:

☆☆☆☆☆

PAGE NO:

MOVIE:

Director:

Date Released:

Written by:

Genre:

Actors:

My Review

MEMORABLE SCENE

MEMORABLE QUOTE

My Rating:
☆☆☆☆☆

PAGE NO:

MOVIE:

Director:

Date Released:

Written by:

Genre:

Actors:

My Review

MEMORABLE SCENE

MEMORABLE QUOTE

My Rating:

☆☆☆☆☆

PAGE NO:

MOVIE:

Director:

Date Released:

Written by:

Genre:

Actors:

My Review

MEMORABLE SCENE

MEMORABLE QUOTE

My Rating:
☆☆☆☆☆

PAGE NO:

MOVIE:

Director:

Date Released:

Written by:

Genre:

Actors:

My Review

MEMORABLE SCENE

MEMORABLE QUOTE

My Rating:
☆☆☆☆☆

PAGE NO:

MOVIE:

Director:

Date Released:

Written by:

Genre:

Actors:

My Review

MEMORABLE SCENE

MEMORABLE QUOTE

My Rating:
☆☆☆☆☆

PAGE NO:

MOVIE:

Director:

Date Released:

Written by:

Genre:

Actors:

My Review

MEMORABLE SCENE

MEMORABLE QUOTE

My Rating:

☆☆☆☆☆

PAGE NO:

MOVIE:

Director:

Date Released:

Written by:

Genre:

Actors:

My Review

MEMORABLE SCENE

MEMORABLE QUOTE

My Rating:

☆☆☆☆☆

PAGE NO:

MOVIE:

Director:

Date Released:

Written by:

Genre:

Actors:

My Review

MEMORABLE SCENE

MEMORABLE QUOTE

My Rating:

☆☆☆☆☆

PAGE NO:

MOVIE:

Director:

Date Released:

Written by:

Genre:

Actors:

My Review

MEMORABLE SCENE

MEMORABLE QUOTE

My Rating:

☆☆☆☆☆

PAGE NO:

MOVIE:

Director:

Date Released:

Written by:

Genre:

Actors:

My Review

MEMORABLE SCENE

MEMORABLE QUOTE

My Rating:

☆☆☆☆☆

PAGE NO:

MOVIE:

Director:

Date Released:

Written by:

Genre:

Actors:

My Review

MEMORABLE SCENE

MEMORABLE QUOTE

My Rating:

☆☆☆☆☆

PAGE NO:

MOVIE:

Director:

Date Released:

Written by:

Genre:

Actors:

My Review

MEMORABLE SCENE

MEMORABLE QUOTE

My Rating:
☆☆☆☆☆

PAGE NO:

MOVIE:

Director:

Date Released:

Written by:

Genre:

Actors:

My Review

MEMORABLE SCENE

MEMORABLE QUOTE

My Rating:

☆☆☆☆☆

PAGE NO:

MOVIE:

Director:

Written by:

Actors:

Date Released:

Genre:

My Review

MEMORABLE SCENE

MEMORABLE QUOTE

My Rating:

PAGE NO:

MOVIE:

Director:

Date Released:

Written by:

Genre:

Actors:

My Review

MEMORABLE SCENE

MEMORABLE QUOTE

My Rating:
☆☆☆☆☆

PAGE NO:

MOVIE:

Director:

Date Released:

Written by:

Genre:

Actors:

My Review

MEMORABLE SCENE

MEMORABLE QUOTE

My Rating:
☆☆☆☆☆

PAGE NO:

MOVIE:

Director:

Date Released:

Written by:

Genre:

Actors:

My Review

MEMORABLE SCENE

MEMORABLE QUOTE

My Rating:
☆☆☆☆☆

PAGE NO:

MOVIE:

Director:

Date Released:

Written by:

Genre:

Actors:

My Review

MEMORABLE SCENE

MEMORABLE QUOTE

My Rating:
☆☆☆☆☆

PAGE NO:

MOVIE:

Director:

Date Released:

Written by:

Genre:

Actors:

My Review

MEMORABLE SCENE

MEMORABLE QUOTE

My Rating:

☆☆☆☆☆

PAGE NO:

MOVIE:

Director:

Date Released:

Written by:

Genre:

Actors:

My Review

MEMORABLE SCENE

MEMORABLE QUOTE

My Rating:

PAGE NO:

MOVIE:

Director:

Date Released:

Written by:

Genre:

Actors:

My Review

MEMORABLE SCENE

MEMORABLE QUOTE

My Rating:
☆☆☆☆☆

PAGE NO:

MOVIE:

Director:

Date Released:

Written by:

Genre:

Actors:

My Review

MEMORABLE SCENE

MEMORABLE QUOTE

My Rating:

☆☆☆☆☆

PAGE NO:

MOVIE:

Director:

Date Released:

Written by:

Genre:

Actors:

My Review

MEMORABLE SCENE

MEMORABLE QUOTE

My Rating:

☆☆☆☆☆

PAGE NO:

MOVIE:

Director:

Date Released:

Written by:

Genre:

Actors:

My Review

MEMORABLE SCENE

MEMORABLE QUOTE

My Rating:

PAGE NO:

MOVIE:

Director:

Date Released:

Written by:

Genre:

Actors:

My Review

MEMORABLE SCENE

MEMORABLE QUOTE

My Rating:
☆☆☆☆☆

PAGE NO:

MOVIE:

Director:

Date Released:

Written by:

Genre:

Actors:

My Review

MEMORABLE SCENE

MEMORABLE QUOTE

My Rating:

☆☆☆☆☆

PAGE NO:

MOVIE:

Director:

Date Released:

Written by:

Genre:

Actors:

My Review

MEMORABLE SCENE

MEMORABLE QUOTE

My Rating:

PAGE NO:

MOVIE:

Director:

Written by:

Actors:

Date Released:

Genre:

My Review

MEMORABLE SCENE

MEMORABLE QUOTE

My Rating:

PAGE NO:

MOVIE:

Director:

Date Released:

Written by:

Genre:

Actors:

My Review

MEMORABLE SCENE

MEMORABLE QUOTE

My Rating:

PAGE NO:

MOVIE:

Director:

Date Released:

Written by:

Genre:

Actors:

My Review

MEMORABLE SCENE

MEMORABLE QUOTE

My Rating:

PAGE NO:

MOVIE:

Director:

Date Released:

Written by:

Genre:

Actors:

My Review

MEMORABLE SCENE

MEMORABLE QUOTE

My Rating:
☆☆☆☆☆

PAGE NO:

MOVIE:

Director:

Date Released:

Written by:

Genre:

Actors:

My Review

MEMORABLE SCENE

MEMORABLE QUOTE

My Rating:

☆☆☆☆☆

PAGE NO:

MOVIE:

Director:

Date Released:

Written by:

Genre:

Actors:

My Review

MEMORABLE SCENE

MEMORABLE QUOTE

My Rating:

☆☆☆☆☆

PAGE NO:

MOVIE:

Director:

Written by:

Actors:

Date Released:

Genre:

My Review

MEMORABLE SCENE

MEMORABLE QUOTE

My Rating:

PAGE NO:

MOVIE:

Director:

Date Released:

Written by:

Genre:

Actors:

My Review

MEMORABLE SCENE

MEMORABLE QUOTE

My Rating:

☆☆☆☆☆

PAGE NO:

MOVIE:

Director:

Date Released:

Written by:

Genre:

Actors:

My Review

MEMORABLE SCENE

MEMORABLE QUOTE

My Rating:
☆☆☆☆☆

PAGE NO:

MOVIE:

Director:

Date Released:

Written by:

Genre:

Actors:

My Review

MEMORABLE SCENE

MEMORABLE QUOTE

My Rating:
☆☆☆☆☆

PAGE NO:

MOVIE:

Director:

Date Released:

Written by:

Genre:

Actors:

My Review

MEMORABLE SCENE

MEMORABLE QUOTE

My Rating:

PAGE NO:

MOVIE:

Director:

Date Released:

Written by:

Genre:

Actors:

My Review

MEMORABLE SCENE

MEMORABLE QUOTE

My Rating:

☆☆☆☆☆

PAGE NO:

MOVIE:

Director:

Date Released:

Written by:

Genre:

Actors:

My Review

MEMORABLE SCENE

MEMORABLE QUOTE

My Rating:

☆☆☆☆☆

PAGE NO:

MOVIE:

Director:

Date Released:

Written by:

Genre:

Actors:

My Review

MEMORABLE SCENE

MEMORABLE QUOTE

My Rating:

PAGE NO:

MOVIE:

Director:

Date Released:

Written by:

Genre:

Actors:

My Review

MEMORABLE SCENE

MEMORABLE QUOTE

My Rating:

☆☆☆☆☆

PAGE NO:

MOVIE:

Director:

Date Released:

Written by:

Genre:

Actors:

My Review

MEMORABLE SCENE

MEMORABLE QUOTE

My Rating:

PAGE NO:

MOVIE:

Director:

Date Released:

Written by:

Genre:

Actors:

My Review

MEMORABLE SCENE

MEMORABLE QUOTE

My Rating:

☆☆☆☆☆

PAGE NO:

MOVIE:

Director:

Date Released:

Written by:

Genre:

Actors:

My Review

MEMORABLE SCENE

MEMORABLE QUOTE

My Rating:

☆☆☆☆☆

PAGE NO:

MOVIE:

Director:

Written by:

Actors:

Date Released:

Genre:

My Review

MEMORABLE SCENE

MEMORABLE QUOTE

My Rating:

☆☆☆☆☆

PAGE NO:

MOVIE:

Director:

Date Released:

Written by:

Genre:

Actors:

My Review

MEMORABLE SCENE

MEMORABLE QUOTE

My Rating:
☆☆☆☆☆

PAGE NO:

MOVIE:

Director:

Date Released:

Written by:

Genre:

Actors:

My Review

MEMORABLE SCENE

MEMORABLE QUOTE

My Rating:

PAGE NO:

MOVIE:

Director:

Date Released:

Written by:

Genre:

Actors:

My Review

MEMORABLE SCENE

MEMORABLE QUOTE

My Rating:
☆☆☆☆☆

PAGE NO:

MOVIE:

Director:

Date Released:

Written by:

Genre:

Actors:

My Review

MEMORABLE SCENE

MEMORABLE QUOTE

My Rating:
☆☆☆☆☆

PAGE NO:

MOVIE:

Director:

Date Released:

Written by:

Genre:

Actors:

My Review

MEMORABLE SCENE

MEMORABLE QUOTE

My Rating:

☆☆☆☆☆

PAGE NO:

MOVIE:

Director:

Date Released:

Written by:

Genre:

Actors:

My Review

MEMORABLE SCENE

MEMORABLE QUOTE

My Rating:

☆☆☆☆☆

PAGE NO:

MOVIE:

Director:

Written by:

Actors:

Date Released:

Genre:

My Review

MEMORABLE SCENE

MEMORABLE QUOTE

My Rating:
☆☆☆☆☆

PAGE NO:

MOVIE:

Director:

Date Released:

Written by:

Genre:

Actors:

My Review

MEMORABLE SCENE

MEMORABLE QUOTE

My Rating:
☆☆☆☆☆

PAGE NO:

MOVIE:

Director:

Date Released:

Written by:

Genre:

Actors:

My Review

MEMORABLE SCENE

MEMORABLE QUOTE

My Rating:

PAGE NO:

MOVIE:

Director:

Date Released:

Written by:

Genre:

Actors:

My Review

MEMORABLE SCENE

MEMORABLE QUOTE

My Rating:

☆☆☆☆☆

PAGE NO:

MOVIE:

Director: _____

Date Released: _____

Written by: _____

Genre: _____

Actors: _____

My Review

MEMORABLE SCENE

MEMORABLE QUOTE

My Rating:
☆☆☆☆☆

PAGE NO:

MOVIE:

Director:

Date Released:

Written by:

Genre:

Actors:

My Review

MEMORABLE SCENE

MEMORABLE QUOTE

My Rating:

PAGE NO:

MOVIE:

Director:

Date Released:

Written by:

Genre:

Actors:

My Review

MEMORABLE SCENE

MEMORABLE QUOTE

My Rating:
☆☆☆☆☆

PAGE NO:

MOVIE:

Director:

Date Released:

Written by:

Genre:

Actors:

My Review

MEMORABLE SCENE

MEMORABLE QUOTE

My Rating:
☆☆☆☆☆

PAGE NO:

MOVIE:

Director:

Date Released:

Written by:

Genre:

Actors:

My Review

MEMORABLE SCENE

MEMORABLE QUOTE

My Rating:
☆☆☆☆☆

PAGE NO:

MOVIE:

Director:

Date Released:

Written by:

Genre:

Actors:

My Review

MEMORABLE SCENE

MEMORABLE QUOTE

My Rating:

☆☆☆☆☆

PAGE NO:

MOVIE:

Director:

Date Released:

Written by:

Genre:

Actors:

My Review

MEMORABLE SCENE

MEMORABLE QUOTE

My Rating:

PAGE NO:

MOVIE:

Director:

Date Released:

Written by:

Genre:

Actors:

My Review

MEMORABLE SCENE

MEMORABLE QUOTE

My Rating:

☆☆☆☆☆

PAGE NO:

MOVIE:

Director:

Date Released:

Written by:

Genre:

Actors:

My Review

MEMORABLE SCENE

MEMORABLE QUOTE

My Rating:

☆☆☆☆☆

PAGE NO:

MOVIE:

Director:

Date Released:

Written by:

Genre:

Actors:

My Review

MEMORABLE SCENE

MEMORABLE QUOTE

My Rating:

☆☆☆☆☆

PAGE NO:

MOVIE:

Director:

Date Released:

Written by:

Genre:

Actors:

My Review

MEMORABLE SCENE

MEMORABLE QUOTE

My Rating:

☆ ☆ ☆ ☆ ☆

PAGE NO:

MOVIE:

Director:

Written by:

Actors:

Date Released:

Genre:

My Review

MEMORABLE SCENE

MEMORABLE QUOTE

My Rating:

⭐⭐⭐⭐⭐

PAGE NO:

MOVIE:

Director:

Date Released:

Written by:

Genre:

Actors:

My Review

MEMORABLE SCENE

MEMORABLE QUOTE

My Rating:
☆☆☆☆☆

PAGE NO:

MOVIE:

Director:

Date Released:

Written by:

Genre:

Actors:

My Review

MEMORABLE SCENE

MEMORABLE QUOTE

My Rating:

☆☆☆☆☆

PAGE NO:

MOVIE:

Director:

Date Released:

Written by:

Genre:

Actors:

My Review

MEMORABLE SCENE

MEMORABLE QUOTE

My Rating:

☆☆☆☆☆

PAGE NO:

MOVIE:

Director:

Date Released:

Written by:

Genre:

Actors:

My Review

MEMORABLE SCENE

MEMORABLE QUOTE

My Rating:

PAGE NO:

MOVIE:

Director:

Date Released:

Written by:

Genre:

Actors:

My Review

MEMORABLE SCENE

MEMORABLE QUOTE

My Rating:
☆☆☆☆☆

PAGE NO:

MOVIE:

Director:

Date Released:

Written by:

Genre:

Actors:

My Review

MEMORABLE SCENE

MEMORABLE QUOTE

My Rating:
☆☆☆☆☆

PAGE NO:

MOVIE:

Director:

Date Released:

Written by:

Genre:

Actors:

My Review

MEMORABLE SCENE

MEMORABLE QUOTE

My Rating:

PAGE NO:

MOVIE:

Director:

Date Released:

Written by:

Genre:

Actors:

My Review

MEMORABLE SCENE

MEMORABLE QUOTE

My Rating:

PAGE NO:

MOVIE:

Director:

Date Released:

Written by:

Genre:

Actors:

My Review

MEMORABLE SCENE

MEMORABLE QUOTE

My Rating:

PAGE NO:

MOVIE:

Director:

Date Released:

Written by:

Genre:

Actors:

My Review

MEMORABLE SCENE

MEMORABLE QUOTE

My Rating:

☆☆☆☆☆

PAGE NO:

MOVIE:

Director:

Date Released:

Written by:

Genre:

Actors:

My Review

MEMORABLE SCENE

MEMORABLE QUOTE

My Rating:

☆☆☆☆☆

PAGE NO:

MOVIE:

Director:

Date Released:

Written by:

Genre:

Actors:

My Review

MEMORABLE SCENE

MEMORABLE QUOTE

My Rating:

☆☆☆☆☆

PAGE NO:

MOVIE:

Director:

Date Released:

Written by:

Genre:

Actors:

My Review

MEMORABLE SCENE

MEMORABLE QUOTE

My Rating:

☆☆☆☆☆

PAGE NO:

Favorite Movies

Title	Main Actor

Favorite Movies

Title	Main Actor

Favorite Movies

Title	Main Actor

Favorite Movies

Title	Main Actor

MOVIE LOAN LOG

Title	Loaned To	Date Taken	Date Returned

MOVIE LOAN LOG

Title	Loaned To	Date Taken	Date Returned

MOVIE LOAN LOG

Title	Loaned To	Date Taken	Date Returned

MOVIE LOAN LOG

Title	Loaned To	Date Taken	Date Returned

Rotten Tomatoes Top 100 Movies of All Time

1. **The Wizard of Oz (1939)**

2. **The Third Man (1949)**

3. **Citizen Kane (1941)**

4. **Das Cabinet des Dr. Caligari. (The Cabinet of Dr. Caligari) (1920)**

5. **All About Eve (1950)**

6. **The Godfather (1972)**

7. **Inside Out (2015)**

8. **Modern Times (1936)**

9. **Metropolis (1927)**

10. **E.T. The Extra-Terrestrial (1982)**

11. **It Happened One Night (1934)**

12. **Singin' in the Rain (1952)**

13. **A Hard Day's Night (1964)**

14. **Boyhood (2014)**

15. **Snow White and the Seven Dwarfs (1937)**

16.   Laura (1944)

17.   North by Northwest (1959)

18.   Repulsion (1965)

19.   The Battle of Algiers (La Battaglia di Algeri) (1967)

20.   King Kong (1933)

21.   The Adventures of Robin Hood (1938)

22.   Rear Window (1954)

23.   Rashômon (1951)

24.   The Maltese Falcon (1941)

25.   Toy Story 3 (2010)

26.   Toy Story 2 (1999)

27.   Selma (2015)

28.   Sunset Boulevard (1950)

29.   The Bride of Frankenstein (1935)

30.   M (1931)

31.   The Philadelphia Story (1940)

32. The Treasure of the Sierra Madre (1948)

33. Taxi Driver (1976)

34. The 400 Blows (Les Quatre cents coups) (1959)

35. Up (2009)

36. Seven Samurai (Shichinin no Samurai) (1956)

37. Bicycle Thieves (Ladri di biciclette) (1949)

38. A Streetcar Named Desire (1951)

39. Zootopia (2016)

40. 12 Angry Men (Twelve Angry Men) (1957)

41. Dr. Strangelove Or How I Learned to Stop Worrying and Love the Bomb (1964)

42. Rebecca (1940)

43. The Night of the Hunter (1955)

44. The Conformist (1970)

45. Frankenstein (1931)

46. Rosemary's Baby (1968)

47. Finding Nemo (2003)

48. The Wrestler (2008)

49. L.A. Confidential (1997)

50. The Hurt Locker (2009)

51. The Babadook (2014)

52. Open City (1946)

53. Tokyo Story (Tôkyô monogatari) (1953)

54. Hell or High Water (2016)

55. The Wages of Fear (1953)

56. The Last Picture Show (1971)

57. Pinocchio (1940)

58. The Grapes of Wrath (1940)

59. Roman Holiday (1953)

60. On the Waterfront (1954)

61. Man on Wire (2008)

62. Toy Story (1995)

63. Anatomy of a Murder (1959)

64. The Leopard (1963)

65. Battleship Potemkin (1925)

66. Annie Hall (1977)

67. Chinatown (1974)

68. Cool Hand Luke (1967)

69. Mr. Turner (2014)

70. The Searchers (1956)

71. The Gold Rush (1925)

72. Before Midnight (2013)

73. The Terminator (1984)

74. Sweet Smell of Success (1957)

75. Short Term 12 (2013)

76. Mary Poppins (1964)

77. Let the Right One In (2008)

78. Shaun the Sheep Movie (2015)

79. The Wild Bunch (1969)

80.   Mud (2013)

81.   Playtime (1973)

82.   The French Connection (1971)

83.   Moonlight (2016)

84.   Love & Friendship (2016)

85.   Invasion of the Body Snatchers (1956)

86.   The Discreet Charm Of The Bourgeoisie (Le Charme Discret de la Bourgeoisie) (1972)

87.   Aliens (1986)

88.   Once Upon a Time in the West (1968)

89.   How to Train Your Dragon (2010)

90.   Leviathan (2014)

91.   Badlands (1974)

92.   Hunt for the Wilder people (2016)

93.   Gloria (2014)

94.   The Manchurian Candidate (1962)

95.   Mean Streets (1973)

96.	8 1/2 (1963)
97.	The Conversation (1974)
98.	Eyes Without a Face (1962)
99.	A Separation (2011)
100.	The Sweet Hereafter (1997)

Printed in Great Britain
by Amazon